Q and A

The little book of questions on.....

HOMEMADE LIQUEURS

Copyright © 2013 Two Magpies Publishing
An imprint of Read Publishing Ltd
Home Farm, 44 Evesham Road, Cookhill, Alcester, Warwickshire, B49 5LJ

Commissioning Editor Rose Hewlett
Words by Sophie Berry
Design and Illustrations by Zoë Horn Haywood

This book is copyright and may not be reproduced or copied in any way without the express permission of the publisher in writing.

British Library Cataloguing-in-Publication Data A catalogue record for this book is available from the British Library.

CONTENTS

Introduction	3
History	7
Equipment	15
Preparation	23
- Cup Measurements	25
Recipes	33
Top Tips and Tricks	72

MAKING LIQUEURS AT HOME IS A WONDERFUL PASTIME!

Making liqueurs at home is a wonderful pastime. Waiting for your liqueur to infuse with your carefully chosen flavour takes a little patience, but we believe it is always worth the wait.

Added to this, the result of making liqueurs at home is often much cheaper than buying them ready-made. By only making what you want, and in quantities you need, there is no waste.

Making liqueurs at home is a wonderful way of using and preserving fruit. During the autumn months especially, when certain fruits are in abundance, making batches

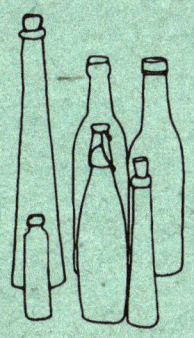

of liqueur to store is a great way to ensure none of the delicious fruits are wasted. Your homemade liqueurs can be stored for many months, allowing you to enjoy your hard work throughout the winter months.

Hopefully you are now feeling inspired to get started on your first batch. This little book will endeavour to answer any questions you have about the liqueur-making process, from how long to leave your liqueur infusing, to how to sterilise your liqueur bottles before use.

ALL THAT'S LEFT TO SAY IS -
GOOD LUCK!

HISTORY

Q. What is liqueur?

A. Liqueurs are alcoholic beverages made from spirits, flavoured with ingredients such as herbs, fruits, spices, nuts, cream.

Q. Where does the word 'liqueur' come from?

A. The word liqueur comes from the Latin word liquifacere which means "to dissolve or melt."

Q. When were the first liqueurs made?

A. The origins of liqueur can be tracked back for centuries. In italy, liqueurs have been produced since the thirteenth century.

Q. What was the earliest liqueur made?

A. Early liqueurs developed from herbal medicines traditionally made by monks. One of the earliest liqueurs is Chartreuse, a naturally green liqueur made from an ancient recipe.

Q. How are liqueurs made?

A. Most liqueurs are made by infusing certain herbs, spices, fruits, or flowers, in either water or alcohol, and sometimes adding sugar, or other flavouring.

Q. How do you consume liqueur? Do you drink it neat?

A. Liqueurs can be enjoyed neat, but also as part of a cocktail.

Q. What do I need to source before making my own liqueur?

A. You will need to source some sealable bottles, or large demijohns to make your liqueur. You can decant your liqueur into smaller bottles to serve from, if you wish.

Q. Is that it?

A. You may also need a small, heavy-bottomed saucepan if your recipe requires you to heat ingredients before adding them to your base spirit.

Q. What is a base spirit?

A. A base spirit is the alcohol that you will steep with your chosen ingredients.

Q. What kind of alcohol do I need to use as a base spirit?

A. Vodka is a popular choice as a base spirit, as it is clear and has no scent, thus lends itself well to being infused with your chosen ingredients.

Q. Can you use spirits other than vodka to make your own liqueurs?

A. Yes, although vodka is a popular choice you can use any spirit you like. Gin, whisky and rum are all popular base spirits.

Q. Will I need any other equipment?

A. Some recipes will require you to filter out the ingredients you have steeped your base spirit with, for example any small pieces of fruit, or herbs. A clean muslin cloth, or coffee filter paper and a funnel will be needed to filter your liqueur.

PREPARATION

Q. Most of the recipes I have seen use cups as a measurement. How much is a cup?

A. You will see that cups are used as measurements in many recipes. A small coffee cup is the best kind to use, and make sure you use the same cup to measure all your ingredients.

Of course, you don't have to use cups. This table is a handy tool if you need to convert cups into other amounts.

CUP MEASURMENTS

1 cup	8 fluid ounces	½ pint	237 ml
2 cups	16 fluid ounces	1 pint	474 ml
4 cups	32 fluid ounces	1 quart	946 ml
2 pints	32 fluid ounces	1 quart	0.946 l
4 quarts	128 fluid ounces	1 gallon	3.784 l

Q. How do I sterilise the bottles I am using for my homemade liqueurs?

A. Sterilisation is simple, but it is is essential that you carry out this task before using your bottles or jars. Simply wash your bottles or jars with very hot soapy water, and rinse with more hot water. Place the bottles or jars into an oven on the lowest heat setting for 20 minutes. Use the bottles or jars when they are still warm.

Q. How long will I need to leave my liqueur to infuse?

A. All homemade liqueur recipes will differ, but on the whole, the longer you leave the liqueur to infuse the better it will taste.

Q. Where should I leave my sealed bottles of liqueur while they infuse?

A. The best place to leave your liqueur to infuse is somewhere cool and dark, like the back of a cupboard.

Q. Is there any way you can speed up the infusing process?

A. If you are infusing your base spirit with sweets, submerging the sealed bottles in hot water or putting them in the dishwasher on a low heat will melt the sweets slightly, helping them release their flavours into your liqueur.

Q. How do I filter my liqueur once it's finished infusing?

A. Simply pour the unfiltered liqueur through a clean muslin cloth or coffee filter paper inside a funnel and into a sterilised bottle for storing. If you are filtering a liqueur with many small ingredients, such as spices, you may want to repeat the process until you are happy with the clarity of your liqueur.

RECIPES

Q. I have heard of sloes, and know you can use them to make homemade liqueur, but what exactly are they?

A. Sloes are from the same fruit-family as plums, and are found in abundance in the English countryside during the autumn months. A little sugar in this recipe helps release the rich sloe juices, and after a few months of infusing, you will be left with a wonderfully warming, syrupy drink. This recipe states to leave the liqueur to infuse for three months, but there is no upper time limit; the longer you can leave it, the better the finished liqueur will taste.

SLOE GIN

INGREDIENTS

1 cup ripe sloes
1 tbsp sugar
3 cups gin

METHOD

1. Carefully prick your sloes with a needle, and place them in a sterilised bottle with the sugar.
2. Top the bottle up with gin, and seal immediately.
3. Leave your liqueur to infuse for a minimum of three months, shaking the bottle every week or so to assist infusion.
4. Serve; no need to strain.

Q. What is Cherry Bounce, and can I make it at home?

A. Cherry Bounce is a delicious liqueur which was originally made in a small village called Frithsden, in England. A lane leading from the Old High Street in the nearby town of Hemel Hempstead is even named Cherry Bounce, in tribute to the sweet liqueur. Using a base spirit of brandy, you can make your own cherry liqueur using this classic recipe

CHERRY BOUNCE

INGREDIENTS

Four cups brandy
1 cup cherries
1 cup sugar

METHOD

1. Stone and pit the cherries, but do not discard the stones.
2. Place the cherries, stones and sugar into a sterilised bottle.
3. Fill the bottle with brandy and quickly seal the bottle.
4. Leave the cherry brandy to infuse for six months; the longer it is left to infuse, the better the taste will be.

Q. Can you make quince liqueur?

A. Yes. The distinctive flavour of quince is a wonderful addition to whisky, creating a rich, malty liqueur. Try this traditional recipe for quince whisky, which makes a perfect warming tipple for a cold evening.

QUINCE WHISKY

INGREDIENTS

1 lb quinces
3 tbsp caster sugar
1 cinnamon stick
1 pint whisky

METHOD

1. Peel and grate the quinces into a large bowl, and sprinkle over 2 tablespoons of the sugar.

2. Leave the quinces and sugar to steep for 24 hours, then strain the juice through a clean muslin cloth, or coffee filter.

3. Add the cinnamon and the rest of the sugar to your quince juice, and pour the mixture into a sterilised bottle.

4. Add the whisky to the bottle, and seal immediately.

5. Leave your liqueur to infuse for three weeks, and filter again using a clean muslin cloth or coffee filter paper before serving.

Q. I'd love to use damsons to make a homemade liqueur. What is a good base spirit to use?

A. Gin is a wonderful base spirit to start with, as it is clear and holds colour well. It's subtle flavour works well with lots of fruits and herbs added, and damson gin is a great recipe to try.

DAMSON GIN

INGREDIENTS

1 lb ripe damsons
4 oz sugar
1 vanilla pod
1 tsp lemon peel
1 cinnamon stick
1 tsp fresh ginger
2 pints gin

METHOD

1. Carefully place all the ingredients into a large sterilised bottle or demijohn, and top up with gin.

2. Seal your bottle immediately.

3. Allow your liqueur to infuse for at least six months; the longer you leave your liqueur to infuse, the stronger the flavour will be.

4. Filter the liquid through a clean muslin cloth or coffee filter paper before decanting into smaller sterilised bottles to serve.

Q. I love Limoncello; is it possible to make it at home?

A. Limoncello is an Italian liqueur, widely enjoyed in Southern Italy. Traditionally, Limoncello is made from the zest of Femminello St. Teresa lemons, also known as Sorrento lemons or Sfusato Lemons. Try this recipe for zesty lemon liqueur, you can use any kind of lemons you like.

LEMON LIQUEUR

INGREDIENTS

Zest of 6 or 7 large organic lemons
1 litre vodka
5 cups water
3 cups sugar

METHOD

1. Carefully peel the zest from the lemons, avoiding the bitter white pith of the lemon skin.
2. Place the zest into a sterilised bottle, topping up with the vodka, and seal immediately.
3. Store the bottled liquid in a cool place and leave to steep for a week.
4. After the 7 days, boil the water and add the sugar to the boiling water. Stir the sugar until it is fully dissolved in the water, and allow the liquid to cool.
5. Strain the lemon peel from the alcohol and discard the peels.
6. Pour the sugar syrup into the glass jar with the alcohol and stir well.
7. Store your liqueur in the fridge.

Q. Is there a simple and straightforward recipe I can try which uses whisky?

A. The sweetness of raspberries work perfectly alongside a whisky base, complementing the malty flavour wonderfully. This recipe for raspberry whisky is an old favourite, and the addition of sugar alongside the fruit makes for a surprisingly sweet liqueur that even non-whisky drinkers will be sure to love.

RASPBERRY WHISKY

INGREDIENTS

2 cups raspberries
1 cup sugar
6 cups whisky

METHOD

1. In a bowl, mash the raspberries and sprinkle the sugar over the top.
2. Cover the bowl with a clean cloth and allow the mixture to stand for 24 hours.
3. Using a square of clean muslin, strain the raspberry mixture to get rid of the seeds.
4. Carefully pour this mixture into a sterilised bottle, topping up the bottle with whisky.
5. Leave the liqueur to infuse for a minimum of three days.

Q. Can you use edible flowers to make homemade liqueur?

A. Edible flowers are a lovely addition to your homemade liqueur, infusing your base spirit with a subtle, aromatic flavour. Wild flowers, such as violets, can be found in abundance at the right time of year, and you can gather handfuls of them for no cost.

VIOLET VODKA

INGREDIENTS

1 cup violets, stems removed
2 cups sugar
4 cups vodka
7 cups cooled, boiled water

METHOD

1. Place the violets into a sterilised bottle with the alcohol and seal immediately. Leave the flowers to infuse for 12 hours.

2. Gently heat the sugar and the water in a small saucepan over a low heat until the sugar has dissolved, and allow the mixture to cool.

3. Remove the violets from the vodka, and using the back of a spoon, crush them into a pulp.

4. Add the violet pulp to the sugar solution and carefully pour this mixture into a bottle to steep for 12 hours.

5. Mix the alcohol and sugar solution together, and filter your liqueur with a clean muslin cloth or coffee filter paper.

6. Bottle and store your liqueur for at least a month before serving.

Q. I'd love to make elderflower liqueur. Is there a really simple recipe I can try at home?

A. Yes, making elderflower liqueur is very simple. Try this recipe. Be aware that the elderflower season is rather short and only lasts the month of June. Get out there early to find the freshest flowers for your infusion.

ELDERFLOWER VODKA

INGREDIENTS

1 cup elderflowers
3 cups vodka

METHOD

1. Simply remove all the stalks and place the flowers into a sterilised bottle and top up with vodka.
2. Leave the liqueur to infuse for a minimum of two weeks, turning the bottles every other day to assist infusion.
3. Carefully strain your liqueur using a clean muslin cloth, or coffee filter paper.
4. Store in a sterilised bottle.

Q. I'd love to make a bold, spicy liqueur. What is a good recipe to start with?

A. Fresh ginger is a fabulously spicy addition to spirits, and works especially well with rum. A dark, spiced rum will really complement the distinctive taste of fresh ginger, or you could use a lighter white rum for a more subtle liqueur.

GINGER RUM

INGREDIENTS

2 tbsp fresh ginger
3 cups rum

METHOD

1. Carefully chop your fresh ginger into chunks. Do not make the chunks too small, and do not remove the skin as it retains a lot of the flavour.

2. Put the chopped ginger into a sterilised bottle.

3. Top up the bottle with the rum, and seal it immediately.

4. Leave the ginger rum to infuse for a minimum of 3 days; the longer it is left, the stronger the flavour will be.

Q. I love the spicy ginger rum recipe, but would like to try make something even spicier...

A. Try using red chillies. The distinctive, fiery flavour of is a daring and delicious addition to vodka, and will leave you with a liqueur with a kick.

CHILLI VODKA

INGREDIENTS

4 cups vodka
4 red chillies

METHOD

1. Simply place your ingredients into a sterilised bottle, and seal immediately.
2. Shake the bottle to blend the ingredients, and leave the liqueur to infuse for a minimum of 7 days.
3. Shake the bottle of liqueur daily, to assist infusion.

Q. Is it possible to infuse homemade liqueur with herbs, or spices?

A. Yes. Herbs are a wonderful addition to your homemade liqueurs, and can add a subtle and aromatic flavour to your final product. Caraway is an herb that has been found in ancient foods, and is still widely used today.

CARAWAY VODKA

INGREDIENTS

4 cups vodka
1 tbsp caraway seeds

METHOD

1. Simply place the seeds into a sterilised bottle and top up with vodka.

2. Leave the liqueur to infuse for a minimum of two weeks, turning the bottles every other day to assist infusion.

3. Carefully strain your liqueur using a clean muslin cloth, or coffee filter paper.

4. Store in a sterilised bottle.

Q. I love aniseed-flavoured liqueur. Is it difficult to make at home?

A. It is very easy to make an anise-infused liqueur at home. It can be consumed neat, or diluted with water as a longer drink, much like the traditional French anise-flavoured aperitif, Pastis.

ANISE LIQUEUR

INGREDIENTS

1/4 cup of green anise seed
1/8 cup coriander seed
4 cups vodka
1/2 tsp cinnamon
1/2 tsp mace

METHOD

1. Place all the ingredients in a sterilised bottle, or bottles.
2. Seal your bottles immediately.
3. Leave your liqueur to infuse in a cool, dark place. A kitchen cupboard is perfect.

Q. Can you use sweets to flavour homemade liqueur?

A. Infusing your spirit with sweets is a fun and innovative way to add flavour and colour to your liqueur. Jelly beans are a great sweet to use, as their vibrant colours and variety of flavours can allow you to make a vast array of liqueurs.

JELLY BEAN VODKA

INGREDIENTS

1 cup jelly beans
4 cups vodka

METHOD

1. Simply place the jelly beans into a sterilised bottle and top up with vodka.

2. Leave the liqueur to infuse for a minimum of two weeks, turning the bottles every other day to assist infusion.

Q. What other sweets can I use to infuse my homemade liqueur?

A. Pear drops are another sweet-shop favourite which work wonderfully as a flavour in homemade liqueurs. Their distinctive flavour, and vibrant colour creates a lovely jewel-toned liqueur which can be enjoyed on its own, or as a long drink when mixed with soda water.

PEAR DROP VODKA

INGREDIENTS

1 cup pear drops
4 cups vodka

METHOD

1. Simply place the pear drops into a sterilised bottle and top up with vodka. Seal the bottle immediately.
2. Leave the liqueur to infuse for a minimum of two weeks, turning the bottles every other day to assist infusion.

Q. Can you make minty liqueur at home?

A. Yes. Adding minty sweets to a vodka base makes for an unusual and delicious liqueur. Mint-infused liqueurs are a quirky and original digestif to offer guests after a meal as an alternative to a classic after-dinner mint. Try this simple recipe for mint vodka which uses mint imperials, the perfect sweet to use to make a refreshing liqueur.

MINT VODKA

INGREDIENTS

1 cup mint imperials
4 cups vodka

METHOD

1. Simply place the mints into a sterilised bottle and top up with vodka. Seal the bottle immediately.
2. Leave the liqueur to infuse for a minimum of two weeks, turning the bottles every other day to assist infusion.

Q. Is it possible to make a nut-infused liqueur at home?

A. Nuts are a fabulous addition to a spirit base, and once steeped, your nut-infused liqueur will make a fantastic ingredient to many a cocktail. We do not recommend eating the nuts after they have been used to infuse your vodka, as they will have absorbed a lot of alcohol.

PEANUT VODKA

INGREDIENTS

1 cups unsalted peanuts
3 cups vodka

METHOD

1. Place your unsalted peanuts into a sterilised bottle.
2. Now, fill the bottle with vodka and quickly seal the top.
3. Leave the vodka to infuse for a minimum of two weeks; the longer the liqueur is left the stronger the flavour will be.
4. Strain the peanuts out of the vodka before serving it.

Q. I love Advocaat, and would like to try making an egg-based liqueur at home. Is there a simple recipe I can try?

A. The addition of eggs will give your liqueur a rich and creamy consistency, and distinctive custard-like flavour. Try this simple recipe for delicious egg-based brandy liqueur.

EGG LIQUEUR

INGREDIENTS

2 egg yolks
2 eggs
4 cups icing sugar
3 cups brandy
5 cups whipping cream

METHOD

1. In a large bowl, whisk the eggs and egg yolks until they are frothy.
2. Sift the powdered sugar into the bowl gradually.
3. Add the alcohol and stir well.
4. Beat the whipping cream until slightly stiff and add this to the egg liqueur.
5. Pour the mixture into a sterilised bottle, and store in the fridge until serving.

Q. Can you infuse liqueur with tea?

A. Flavouring a base spirit with tea is a great way to infuse your liqueur with a subtle taste and distinctive aroma. As the flavours are already encased in a tea bag, you will not need to filter or strain your liqueur before you drink it, you can simply remove the bags.

EARL GREY GIN

INGREDIENTS

4 Earl Grey tea bags
4 cups gin

METHOD

1. Simply place your tea bags in sterilised bottles, and top up with the gin.//
2. Seal the bottles immediately, and set aside somewhere cool.
3. Leave your liqueur to infuse for 6-8 hours. Do not leave for longer than 8 hours, or the liqueur may take on a bitter taste.
4. Remove the tea bags. Your liqueur is now ready to serve.

Q. Is there a simple recipe I can try for a festive homemade liqueur?

A. Yes. A cranberry-based liqueur, complemented with a Christmas spice such as cinnamon is a perfect festive beverage, and once decanted into little bottles makes a thoughtful and original gift. Try this simple recipe for spiced Christmas liqueur.

CHRISTMAS LIQUEUR

INGREDIENTS

6 oz sugar
4 oz cinnamon sticks, bruised
4 cups whisky

METHOD

1. Simply place your ingredients into a sterilised bottle, and seal immediately.
2. Shake the bottle to blend the ingredients, and leave the liqueur to infuse for a minimum of 10 days.
3. Shake the bottle of liqueur daily, to assist infusion.
4. Carefully filter your liqueur with a clean muslin cloth or coffee filter paper.

TOP TEN TIP

1. Baby sterilising powder is a failsafe method of ensuring your bottles are safe to use

2. Making batches of liqueur throughout the year means you will always have a supply of homemade liqueur available.

3. Prepare in advance. If you need your liqueur ready for a particular occasion check the recipe well in advance and make sure you leave plenty of time for infusion.

4. Using seasonal fruits in your liqueur is a great way of utilising and preserving fruits when in abundance.

5. When using boiled sweets to infuse your base spirit, you can speed up the process dramatically by using a dishwasher. Put your sealed bottles in the dishwasher on a low heat, and the heat from the water will melt the sweets slightly, releasing their flavour and colour into the base spirit. Allow to cool thoroughly before consuming and be sure to use a low heat or the glass may shatter.

...AND TRICKS

6. If you don't have a dishwasher, you can use a bowl of very hot water to help speed up infusion. Submerge the bottles in hot water until the water has cooled. Allow to cool thoroughly before consuming.

7. For best results in liqueur making, store your bottles in a cool, dark place out of direct sunlight. This will also allow them to keep for much longer.

8. Be on the lookout for decorative decanters and dainty little liqueur glasses to serve your liqueur in; secondhand shops and antique fairs are a good place to look.

9. Personalise your glass bottles with a handwritten label to make a bottle of homemade liqueur into a wonderful gift.

10. Always enjoy your homemade liqueur in moderation.

NOTES

NOTES

Image Credits

All Pages - This work is a derivative of "Textures: Paper IMG_0006" is Copyright ©2007-2012 ~Dioma, made available on DeviantArt under Creative Commons Attribution 2.0 Generic (CC BY 2.0) http://dioma.deviantart.com/art/Textures-Paper-58028330

All Pages - This work is a derivative of "Textures: Paper IMG_0002" is Copyright ©2007-2012 Dioma, made available on DeviantArt under Creative Commons Attribution 2.0 Generic (CC BY 2.0) http://dioma.deviantart.com/art/Textures-Paper-58028330

All Chapter Pages - This work is a derivative of "Frame back" is copyright © 2009 Sunset Sailor made available on Flickr under Creative Commons Attribution 2.0 Generic (CC BY 2.0) http://www.flickr.com/photos/sunsetsailor/3558408492

Page 2-3 - This work is a derivative of "Liqueur" is copyright © 2009 Kim Love, lovelihood, made available on Flickr under Creative Commons Attribution 2.0 Generic (CC BY-SA 2.0) http://www.flickr.com/photos/lovelihood/4069506605/sizes/o/in/photostream/

Pages 6-7 - This work is a derivative of "Bottles of homemade strawberry liqueur" is copyright © 2004 By Blue Lotus, made available on Wikimedia Commons and Flickr, under Creative Commons Attribution 2.0 Generic (CC BY-SA 2.0), http://www.flickr.com/photos/bluelotus/18313725/

Page 14-15 - This work is a derivative of "Pots and Pans" is copyright © 2012 jeeheon made available on Flickr under Creative Commons Attribution 2.0 Generic (CC BY 2.0) http://www.flickr.com/photos/jeeheon/7877017204

Pages 22-23 - This work is a derivative of "Kitchen Tools at the Table" is copyright © 2012, slightly everything, Kate Hiscock, made available on Flickr under Creative Commons Attribution 2.0 Generic (CC BY 2.0) http://www.flickr.com/photos/slightlyeverything/8229722025

Page 31 - This work is a derivative of "Blueberry #2" is copyright © 2009 Willrad, Willrad von Doomenstein, made available on Flickr under Creative Commons Attribution 2.0 Generic (CC BY-SA 2.0) http://www.flickr.com/photos/willrad/3810599140/

Pages 32-33 - This work is a derivative of "Everclear vs. Vodka" is copyright © 2009 Willrad, Willrad von Doomenstein, made available on Flickr under Creative Commons Attribution 2.0 Generic (CC BY 2.0) http://www.flickr.com/photos/willrad/3760187068/in/photostream/

www.ingramcontent.com/pod-product-compliance
Lightning Source LLC
Chambersburg PA
CBHW062120080426
42734CB00012B/2930